South De
Dog Walks

Robert Hesketh

Bossiney Books · Exeter

First published 2023 by
Bossiney Books Ltd, 68 Thorndale Courts, Whitycombe Way,
Exeter, EX4 2NY
www.bossineybooks.com

ISBN 978-1906474-98-0

Acknowledgements
The maps are by Graham Hallowell
All photographs are by the author, www.roberthesketh.co.uk

Printed in Great Britain by Deltor, Satash, PL12 6LZ

All the walks in this book were checked prior to publication, at
which time the instructions were correct. However, changes can
occur in the countryside over which neither the author nor
the publisher has any control. Please let us know
if you encounter any serious problems.

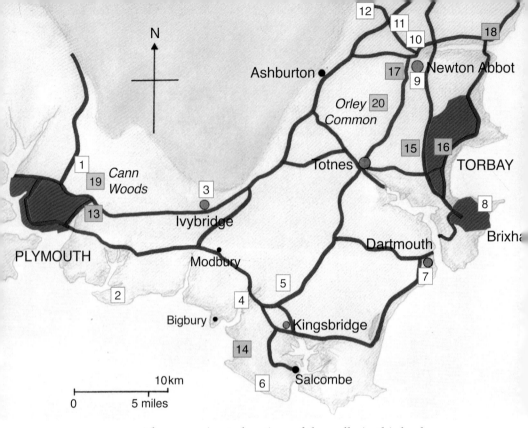

The approximate locations of the walks in this book

Introduction

These walks have been chosen with dogs in mind. All have off-lead opportunities and most have water for dogs to play in. We've avoided difficult stiles and potential hazards such as unfenced cliffs and busy roads – many routes are off-road altogether.

They range from a short run up to a half day's circuit of 6.8 km (4¹/₄ miles), so the time needed to complete them will vary too. Every walk has its individual character and there are many wonderful viewpoints and places of interest for us humans as well as our canine friends to linger over on the way.

The countryside

Walking is safe and healthy exercise for both people and dogs, but beware of rising tides and strong currents. Devon rivers can rise fast and water that's normally safe for your dog can become hazardous after heavy rain. Please leave farm gates closed or open as you find them. Finally, please heed warning signs and keep your dog on a lead near livestock, especially during the lambing and bird nesting season. Dogs are instinctual hunters. Although they may not kill, they can drive nesting birds from their broods, worry livestock and cause sheep to drop their lambs.

On Access Land, which includes Orley Common and the Coastpath sections in this book, it is a legal requirement to keep your dog on a lead no more than 2 metres long between 1 March and 31 July, and at all times around livestock.

Footwear and clothing

Walking is a pleasure throughout the seasons so long as you're prepared. Mud and puddles are par for the course. Walking boots are ideal, but sandals inadequate, whilst Wellingtons don't breathe or provide ankle support. Devon's weather can change suddenly and it most certainly rains, so it's wise to bring extra layers of clothing plus a waterproof. On some paths there may be gorse or nettles, therefore trousers are preferable to shorts, especially as they provide some protection against ticks which may carry debilitating Lyme disease and are intensely irritating. If a tick attaches itself to you or your dog, remove it promptly and carefully with tweezers.

Extras

Drinking water is a must for people and dogs – you'll soon need it and dehydration causes tiredness, especially in hot weather. Indeed, very hot weather is best avoided, especially if your pet has a thick coat. I recommend walking poles or a stick too and a mobile phone and GPS device if you have them. The sketch maps in this book are just that – sketches. You may want to carry the relevant OS Explorer for extra information. Finally, please remember to bring dog poo bags (preferably biodegradable) and dispose of them properly.

How to get there

We have given OS 6-figure grid references, and what3words references, as well as driving directions.

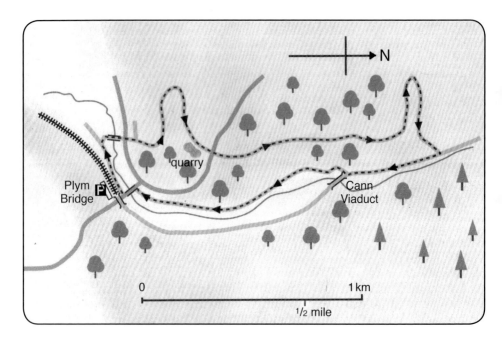

Walk 1   Plym Bridge Woods

Distance: 3.8km (2¹/₂ miles)
*Character: This delightful off-lead walk is on Plymouth's doorstep,
yet hidden from the city. It follows woodland and riverbank paths,
with several swimming places for dogs. Part of the route uses a
section of former tramway with granite sleepers. Another section
follows the old South Devon and Tavistock Railway (1859),
including Cann Viaduct, from where nesting peregrines may be
seen. There are dog bins at the start.*

Start from the National Trust's Plym Bridge Woods car park
(SX 524586, ///splice.page.silks) which is signed on roads from
Plympton. Use the map in the car park to orient yourself. Turn left
out of the car park and under the stone railway bridge, part of the
Plym Valley Railway, which runs vintage steam- and diesel-hauled
trains. Turn immediately left onto the riverbank path. Bear right
when the path divides and cross the footbridge.

   Immediately cross the lane and head uphill on a short tarred
track. Turn right up a stony path at the end of the track, keeping a
stream on your right. Turn right along a raised embankment when

4

you reach a T junction. This has stone tramway sleepers, some still bearing the original iron spikes. Continue on the embankment as the track curves right. Go through a kissing gate to a lane. Cross and continue over a footbridge and on along the broad, level path ahead. Ignore side turnings. Again, look out for stone tramway sleepers.

The track curves left along the contour. Bear right down a broad path just beyond the top of the curve. Continue across another path and on downhill with the stream on your right.

Turn right when you meet the tarred cycle track. Continue to Cann Viaduct, where the RSPB have telescopes trained on peregrines nesting on the quarry face opposite. Helpful staff are happy to tell visitors about the peregrines and the many other bird species seen here.

Retrace your steps to the end of the viaduct and turn left, then turn right onto the bankside path. Follow this to Plym Bridge. Cross it and retrace your steps to the start.

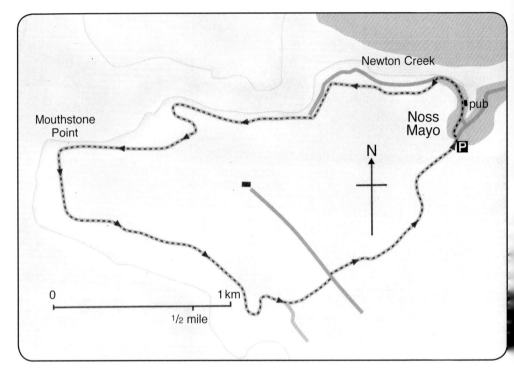

Walk 2 Noss Mayo

Distance: 6.8 km/4 1/4 miles

Character: This beautiful walk gives superb views of Newton Creek, the Yealm estuary and the coast. Apart from a gentle descent at the end, there are no steep slopes as most of the walk follows Revelstoke Drive, a nine mile long carriage drive created in the 1880s by the banker Edward Baring, Lord Revelstoke.

Take binoculars: you may spot seals and dolphins around Warren Point and seabirds wheeling over the cliffs. Parts of the walk are off-lead, but please observe signs and keep your dog leashed near livestock.

Start from Noss Mayo car park in Hannaford Road (SX 547474, ///composts.character.stars). Leave the car park, cross the lane and walk ahead, following FOUNDRY LANE to the foot of the rise. Turn left, SHIP INN. The Ship is a charming dog-friendly pub overlooking Newton Creek. It has a great collection of local period photos and nautical memorabilia.

Continue along the lane, which curves left. Turn left up steps, FORDHILL PLANTATION. Follow the footpath ahead parallel to the lane. Continue until the path dips to rejoin the lane. Walk ahead, COAST PATH THE WARREN. The path soon divides: keep right.

The footpath joins a stony track. Keep left when the track divides (the path right leads only to the beach). Continue to a gate. Please leash your dog now as there is livestock in neighbouring fields. Continue along the Coastpath (Revelstoke Drive) by Mouthstone Point. Continue as the Coastpath turns south and then east.

Keep left at a fingerpost, PUBLIC FOOTPATH WARREN NOSS MAYO. Reaching a lane, turn left, then turn right after 40m, PUBLIC FOOTPATH NOSS MAYO. Enjoy a fine view over to Dartmoor as the stony track descends to the car park.

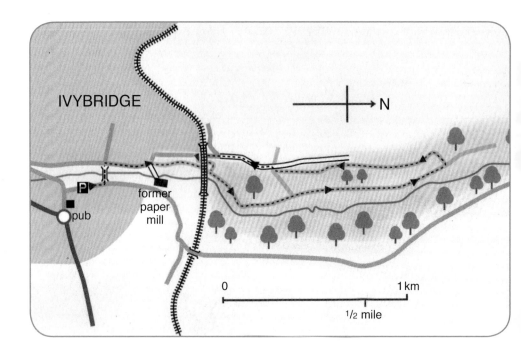

Walk 3 Ivybridge Longtimber Woods

Distance: 3.5km (2¹/₄ miles)
Character: The beautiful riverbank path beside the wooded river Erme is a classic dog walk. However, although there are relatively quiet pools for dogs to swim in, please remember the Erme is a fast flowing river with a rocky bed and is really dangerous when in spate. This route passes by the former Stowford Mill of 1862 and under the towering viaduct of the GWR mainline.

Sir James Inglis built the present structure of eight granite and brick arches in 1893, but the granite piers of IK Brunel's 1848 timber viaduct are alongside. Also on the way is a former pound and reservoir.

The return is through woods via an old leat, the King's Gutter, cut in 1818. Apart from the start and a short lane section, this walk is off-lead. One short steep ascent and descent.

Unless you can find one of the limited parking places on Station Road, start from Harford Road car park (SX 636563, ///crunches. jeering.deflate). Follow the path upriver and cross the packhorse

8

bridge, built in the 17th century and later widened. Turn right into STATION ROAD. Take the PUBLIC FOOTPATH by the entrance to former Stowford Mill.

Continue under the railway viaduct to a path junction. Turn right and follow the path upriver. Ignore the first PUBLIC FOOTPATH left. Continue upriver.

Take the next PUBLIC FOOTPATH left and uphill. Cross a rough path and continue uphill to meet PUBLIC FOOTPATH by a stone wall. Turn left, following the path beside the stone wall.

Reaching a lane, turn left. Ignore the footpath which turns sharp left 40 m ahead. Follow the lane downhill, passing under the viaduct. Almost immediately, turn sharp left onto the footpath to loop back under the viaduct. Turn right (PUBLIC FOOTPATH) and retrace your steps to the start.

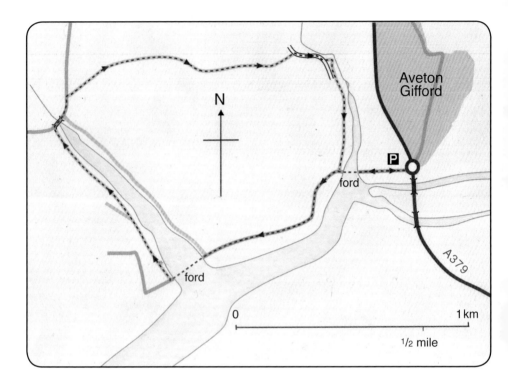

Walk 4 Aveton Gifford

Distance: 3.6 km (2 1/4 miles)
Character: This very scenic walk follows the tidal Avon before turning inland beside a creek. Climbing a green lane, it offers fine views over the South Hams, before descending to the estuary. Much of the route is off-lead. Bring binoculars to watch waders and wildfowl. Before starting, please check the tide times and avoid the period two hours either side of high tide (three hours on spring tides) as the tidal section floods.

Start from the signed free car park (SX 692472, ///toddler.learning. haggling) by the roundabout just outside Aveton Gifford on the A379 Kingsbridge road. Use the display map to orient yourself. Turn right out of the car park to follow the tidal road beside the estuary and across a ford. Continue to a second ford. If the tide is high, turn immediately right and follow the footpath along the eastern bank of the creek to rejoin the directions at *.

Otherwise, if the tide is out, cross this ford and turn immediately right (PUBLIC FOOTPATH) along the western bank of the creek behind a lime kiln. Bear right when the path joins another path. Meeting a lane, turn right.

Cross a small bridge*. Ignore the turning immediately right (unless you came by the eastern bank). Turn right, PUBLIC BYWAY DRUNKARD'S HILL UNSUITABLE FOR VEHICLES. This climbs steeply. Fine views over the rolling green hills open out.

Reaching a stile, fork right (PUBLIC FOOTPATH) across a field to a second stile. Continue in the same direction downhill across a large field, over a third stile to a tarred bridleway. Turn right and then left (PUBLIC FOOTPATH) down steps and over a stile. Follow this footpath to meet the tidal road at the western end of the first ford. Retrace your steps to the start.

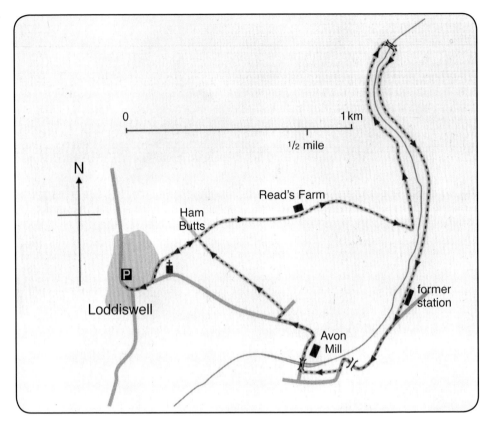

Walk 5 Loddiswell

Distance: 5.3km (3¼ miles)

Character: This walk explores a beautiful section of the Avon valley from Loddiswell, a hilltop village with a historic church and a dog-friendly inn. Much of the route is off-lead, with opportunities for your dog to swim in the river. Part of the walk follows the former 'Primrose Line', the railway that linked Kingsbridge and the Avon Valley to the main line at South Brent until closure in 1963. It is particularly lovely in spring, with many wildflowers in the woods, and in autumn as the leaves turn colour. There is one steep ascent and descent.

Loddiswell is 5km (3 miles) north of Kingsbridge on the B3196. Start from Loddiswell's signed car park (SX719486, ///juggles. inclines.steepest).

Turn right and immediately left, and left again 20 m ahead. Head

12

towards the church. Take the walled lane left of the church. Ignore UNMETALLED ROAD on your right. Reaching HAM BUTTS, continue ahead (READ'S FARM) down the farm track.

Turn right (PUBLIC FOOTPATH) just before Read's Farm. Please heed signs and put your dog on a lead over the farmland. The footpath leads downhill with a brook on the left. Cross the brook by a footbridge. Continue downhill with the brook on your right. Turn left (PUBLIC FOOTPATH), leaving the field and continuing on the bankside footpath. You can now let your dog off its lead. Cross a footbridge on your left and continue upriver.

Turn right over the former Silveridge Bridge, then right down the opposite bank, following the course of the disused railway. The old goods yard office is now a small photography gallery and has press cuttings about the Primrose Line and Loddiswell station.

Join the lane by the former station entrance and turn right, following the lane under the old railway bridge. Join a PUBLIC FOOTPATH on the right across a field. Turn left onto the lane and cross the bridge. Continue past Avon Mill with its garden centre, café and deli and up the lane, which climbs steeply.

Turn right, CLOVERWELL FARM. Only 40m ahead, turn left, UNMETALLED ROAD. Follow this uphill to HAM BUTTS, turn left and retrace your steps to the car park.

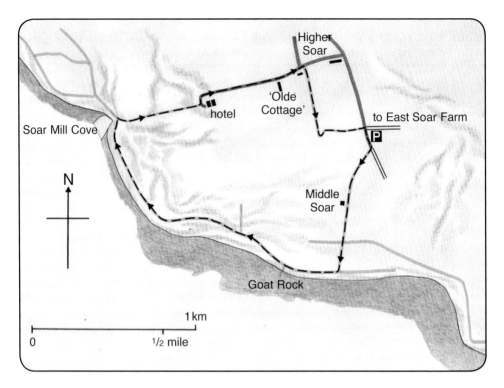

Walk 6   Soar Mill Cove

Distance: 5.4km (3¹/2 miles)
Character: Soar Mill Cove is set amid beautiful coastal scenery.
A delightful, sandy, dog-friendly beach, it is usually much quieter
than better known South Devon beaches.

Start from the National Trust's East Soar car park (SX713375, ///rafters.alas.studs). To drive there, take the Salcombe road (A381). At Malborough, turn right, GALMPTON BOLBERRY SOAR. Just past the church, keep left (BOLBERRY SOAR), then follow the signs for SOAR. At a crossing, by former coastguard cottages, continue ahead to the car park.

From the car park, continue ahead on the lane by which you arrived, LINK TO COASTPATH SOAR MILL COVE. After 100m, turn right PUBLIC FOOTPATH. Skirt around Middle Soar as signed and continue ahead. At a path crossing you may either turn right (SOAR MILL COVE) to take the inland path to the cove, or walk ahead (LINK TO THE COASTPATH) and then turn right.

14

The Coastpath route is particularly beautiful, but you should leash your dog after 750 m/¹/₂ mile when it descends steeply towards Steeple Cove as there are unfenced cliffs from there to Soar Mill Cove.

Reaching Soar Mill Cove by either route, divert left for the beach. To return to the start you may either retrace your steps or, to make a circular walk, turn right MALBOROUGH and ascend steadily. Keep left when the path divides. At a gate turn left onto the lane, or divert right to dog-friendly Soar Mill Cove Hotel. Continue past the hotel car park and Lower Soar, with its attractive thatched Olde Cottage. Ignore PUBLIC FOOTPATH LINK TO COASTPATH.

Turn right (PUBLIC FOOTPATH) where several lanes and tracks meet at Higher Soar. Continue past two gates. Keep your dog on a lead as signed and walk ahead along the field edge ahead to the field corner. Turn left. Turn right at the yellow waymark 100 m ahead, round a tight dog-leg, then continue south-south-east as signed, along the grassy bank that leads to a small gate. Go through the gate. Walk ahead 50 m to another waymark. Turn left on the path. Retrace your steps to the car park.

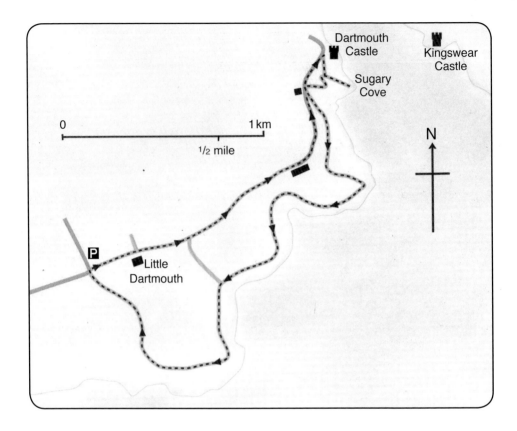

Walk 7 Little Dartmouth

Distance: 5.8 km (3³/₄ miles) or 4.9 km (3 miles)
Character: This stimulating coastal walk offers wonderful views and is mainly off-lead. The full route includes two dog-friendly coves and Dartmouth's fascinating castle, medieval but rearmed and updated over the centuries (English Heritage, admission charge, dogs permitted on leads). There are some steep, stepped sections, especially on the paths to the coves.

Start from the National Trust's Little Dartmouth car park (SX874492, ///buzzards.graceful.begins), signed from the A379 between Dartmouth and Stoke Fleming. Use the car park's map to orient yourself. Take BRIDLEWAY DARTMOUTH CASTLE, but please keep your dog leashed until you pass Little Dartmouth Farm. Continue ahead for DARTMOUTH at the path junction. Ignore the next footpath on the right and continue ahead on the green lane.

Ignore the steep path right (unless you wish to take a short cut). Continue ahead past coastguard cottages. Now a tarred track, the bridleway descends. Look across the Dart estuary for a fine view of Kingswear Castle and the Daymark, 24m high and built in 1864.

Reaching Compass Cottage, you may take a short cut back to the start by turning right (COAST PATH LITTLE DARTMOUTH) and following directions from*. For the full route, which includes two dog-friendly coves and Dartmouth Castle, but also steep slopes and steps, continue ahead, then turn immediately right, COASTPATH.

Take the next turn right after only 100m and follow the corkscrew path down to Sugary Cove. Start retracing your steps up the path. Turn right at the top of the first flight of steps. Meeting a lane, turn right (DARTMOUTH CASTLE) down steps. Turn right for the castle entrance or sharp right for tiny Castle Cove. Retrace your steps to the lane. Continue ahead on the lane, LITTLE DARTMOUTH.

* Turn left (COASTPATH LITTLE DARTMOUTH) at Compass Cottage. Continue ahead at a fingerpost, COASTPATH LITTLE DARTMOUTH. (The path to Compass Cove was closed at the time of writing due to slippage). The path climbs steeply, then divides. Bear left.

At the next fingerpost you can take short cut PERMISSIVE LINK NATIONAL TRUST CAR PARK. Otherwise, continue ahead, COASTPATH. At the next fingerpost, the path turns inland to the start.

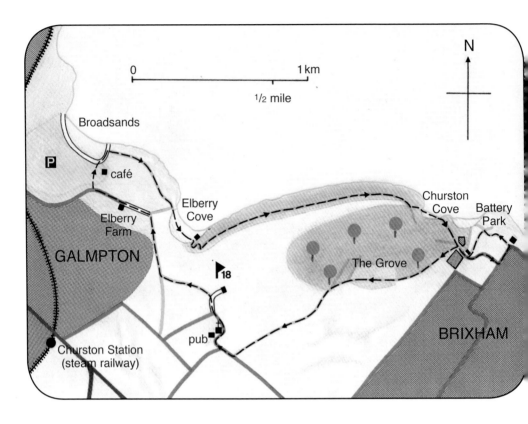

Walk 8 Churston Ferrers

Distance: 5 km (3 miles) Time: 1¹/₂ hours
Character: This mainly off-lead walk includes three beaches: two
permit dogs all year, one has a summer dog ban. Much of it follows
the Coastpath, with fine views across Torbay. Apart from a short
lane section, the rest of the route consists of woodland and field
paths. There are dog bins between the start and Elberry Cove.

Churston Ferrers is signed from the Paignton to Brixham road.
Park carefully on the lane near Churston Court Hotel, a dog-
friendly Grade 1 listed building (SX 904564, ///laugh.marmalade.
dates). Follow the lane around the church and up a slope. Continue
on a private road (BROADSANDS) and then on a path, ELBERRY COVE.
Please put your dog on a lead across the golf course. Follow the
yellow posts into a path.

Ignore the first path on your right. Turn right only a few metres

ahead down a second path. Turn left after 300 m at a path junction (unless you want to turn right and take a short cut to Elberry Cove). Walk on past Elberry Farm.

Turn right to the beach (dogs permitted between October and April); pass the beach huts then turn right again along the Coastpath to Elberry Cove. At the far end of the beach is the ruin of Lord Churston's bathhouse, where he took a hot bath, followed by a cold plunge.

Follow the path up steps to a fork. Keep left along the Coastpath, passing behind the golf course. Turn left and descend steps to Churston Cove. Cross it and continue uphill to a fingerpost. You may divert left here to visit Battery Park and dog friendly Fishcombe Cove with its toilets and café.

For the main route, continue ahead, GREENWAY VIA CHURSTON FERRERS. The path leads gently uphill, then up a few steps. Follow signs for CHURSTON FERRERS at path junctions. Reaching a lane, turn right and right again to the start.

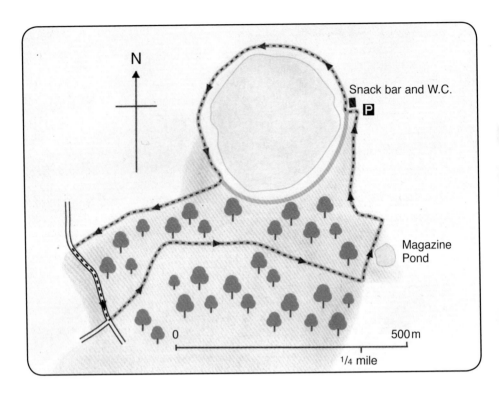

N

Snack bar and W.C.

Magazine
Pond

0

500m

1/4 mile

Walk 9   Decoy Park, Newton Abbot

Distance: 2km (1¹/₄) miles
Character: Decoy was once a clay quarry. Now a country park with
a snack kiosk, ranger's office, toilets and children's play park, it has
been re-colonised by nature. Surrounded by woodland and heath,
Decoy is criss-crossed with footpaths and has two lakes which attract
a variety of wildfowl, including gulls, mallard and swans. Please
follow the signs and keep you dog out of the water and on a lead for
the first half of the lakeside path.

Decoy Park (SX866703, ///king.chats.cans) is signed from the
Sainsbury's supermarket, Newton Abbot. Consult the wall map at
the start. Three trails are marked. The Blue Trail (1.2km, ³/₄ mile)
is a simple circuit of the main lake; the Red Trail at 2.4km, 1¹/₂
miles includes more woodland and the Green Trail (3.2km, 2
miles) has a larger woodland extension.

  With several signed paths there are a number of possibilities:
the route given here is an adaptation of the Red and Green Trails

designed to include both lakes and some pretty woodland paths, whilst avoiding the areas most prone to flooding. However, Decoy is in a low lying clay basin, so expect some mud on the woodland tracks!

Turn right along the lakeside path. Reaching a path junction at the far side of the lake, turn sharp right onto the signed Red Trail. Continue ahead at the next waymark on the Green Trail through a kissing gate. Continue along the field edge.

Turn left, PUBLIC FOOTPATH. This leads along a farm track. Turn left, PUBLIC FOOTPATH. Keep left when the path divides. Turn left at the next waymark, by a helpful map.

Walk down the steps to the Magazine Pond, which takes its name from the former explosives store (magazine) nearby. Turn left at the next waymark and follow the Red Trail around the edge of the football pitch. Continue to the start.

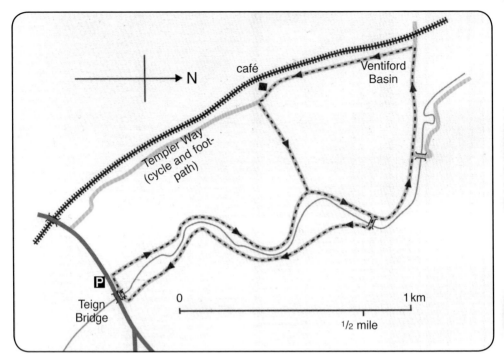

Walk 10 Teign Bridge to Ventiford Basin

Distance: 5.4km (3¹/₂ miles) or 2.4km (1¹/₂miles)

Character: This level riverbank and field path route is off road and off-lead, except where there is livestock. Dogs will enjoy the river, but beware: the current is strong in places and very strong after heavy rain. Watch for birds, including ducks, egrets and also sand martins nesting in the riverbanks.

Start from the car park on the south side of the road by Teign Bridge (SX859734, ///lobbed.conducted.adventure), two miles north of Newton Abbot on the minor road between Whitehill and Sandygate. Cross the road and walk through a metal gate. Follow the riverbank path.

Reaching a waymark, continue ahead to a metal bridge. Fine views to Dartmoor open out. At this point you could cross the bridge and follow the directions from * to the start, thus reducing the walk by 3km.

For the full route, continue ahead on the riverbank path. Continue along the path as it diverges from the river to meet the Templer Way at Ventiford Basin.

Do not follow the cycle track south from Ventiford. Take the parallel footpath along the now dry canal. This later rejoins the cycle track. Continue past a canal lock. Cross the bridge if you wish to visit the adjoining café. Otherwise, turn right and continue for 100 m. Turn left (HERITAGE TRAIL) at a kissing gate. Follow the path across fields to the waymark encountered earlier.

*Follow the riverbank path upriver to the first bridge. Cross, climb steps and turn right down the riverbank track. Continue as the path diverges from the track. Continue ahead at a footpath junction. Cross the new footbridge opposite the stone built road bridge (1815) to the start.

Part of the route follows the disused Stover Canal (1790-92). This carried cut granite from Haytor Quarries on Dartmoor by a granite tramway, a section of which can be seen at Ventiford Basin, along with a tram truck and a hand-operated crane. Plaques explain its history.

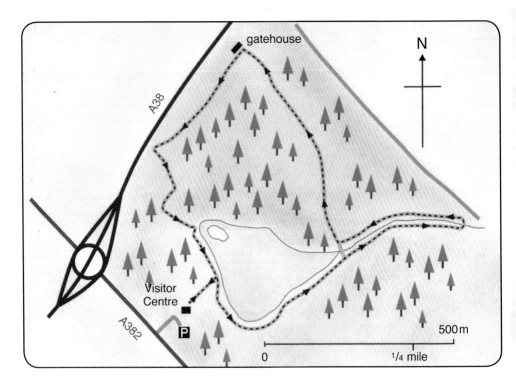

Walk 11 Stover Country Park

Distance: 2.7 km/1³/₄ miles
Character: This delightful nature reserve, noted for its bird and insect life, is criss-crossed with paths and popular with dog walkers; dog bins are provided. Enjoy an easy, level walk by lakeside and woodland paths, but please keep your dog on a lead by the lake and watercourses. Bring binoculars for birdwatching.

Stover Country Park is signed from the A382, 3 miles north of Newton Abbot. From the car park (SX 832750, ///departure.aviation.deflection), head to the visitor centre (free map guides and toilets). Follow the HERITAGE TRAIL to the lake. Turn right along the lakeside path. Continue on the path as it turns left. Turn right up the aerial walkway (opposite bird feeder). Return to the lakeside path and turn right. Continue past a plaque explaining the work of the Canadian Forestry Corps.

Turn almost immediately right (HERITAGE TRAIL VENTIFORD) and follow the path along the watercourse. Turn left over a footbridge and left again along the far side of the watercourse.

24

Turn right on reaching the lake, TO THE GATEHOUSE. Continue ahead at a path junction to view the gatehouse which was built in 1830 to serve the driveway to Stover House; it is Grade II* listed.

Facing the gatehouse, turn left down a minor path. Follow the path when it turns left. Reaching a tarred track (the Stover Trail), turn right. Continue as the track turns left. At the lakeside path turn right over a footbridge and follow the path left. Turn right and retrace your steps to the start.

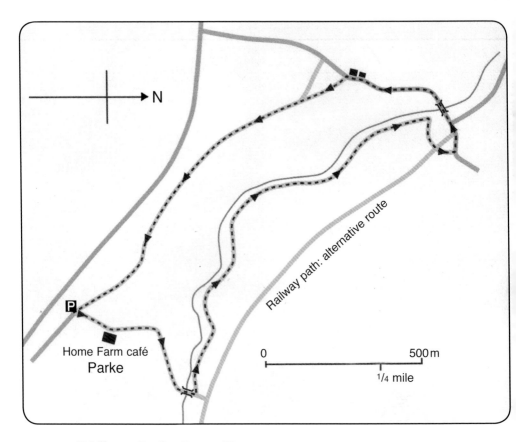

Walk 12   Parke, Bovey Tracey

Distance: 3.2 km (2 miles) Time: 1 hour
Character: This walk explores the beautiful Parke Estate by river-
bank, woodland and field paths. Apart from a short lane section it is
off-lead and especially popular with water-loving dogs – but please
beware: the River Bovey rises fast after heavy rain. This may make
the river unsafe for dogs and flood the riverbank path, but the parallel
railway path offers a dry alternative. There is a dog-friendly café
near the start and a single dog bin.

Start from the National Trust car park (SX805785, ///cans.alcove.
haystack) at Parke , signed from the Haytor Road B3387 just outside Bovey Tracey. Head downhill (DISABLED DROP OFF) by the helpful map. Continue past the orchard and café, heading downhill.
Cross the river Bovey by a stone bridge.

Turn left along the riverbank path for 1 km (³/₄ mile), ignoring side turnings. Continue on the path when it turns right away from the river and climbs to meet the railway path. Bear left down to the lane and put your dog on its lead.

Cross under the bridge. Ignore the turn right (LUSTLEIGH) and continue over the river bridge. Follow the lane uphill. Turn left opposite a late Victorian gatehouse. Go through a gate and keep right when the path forks ahead. Turn right and uphill at the next path junction. Turn left at the following path junction. Follow the high level path to a field gate.

Keep to the left hand path through the centre of the field (please put your dog on a lead if there are livestock). Go through double gates into the next field. Continue along the right field edge and into an enclosed path. Continue to the start.

There and back walks

Walk 13   Saltram

Saltram Park is owned by the National Trust and open from dawn to dusk. Walking the pleasant, dog-friendly trails is free, although there is an admission charge for visiting the house and gardens and using the National Trust car park (SX 522555, ///code.save.circle). The main entrance is well signed from Plympton. Alternatively, use the free parking area (SX505543) at Chelson Meadow, signed 'Plymouth Recycling Centre, Chelson Meadow' from the A379 (Plymstock road by Laira Bridge).

Follow the footpath by the Plym estuary for 700m to enter Saltram Park by a small beach. Use the large display map to orient yourself. The Riverside Walk is rated 'easy' at one hour; the Dell and Boundary Walks 'moderate' at 3/4 hour. Parts of these walks are shared with cyclists. The Trust asks dog owners to observe signs about keeping dogs under control and on a lead.

Walk 14 South Milton Sands

South Milton Sands is well signed from the A381 Kingsbridge/
Salcombe road. It is continuous with Thurlestone Sands, which
gives 700 m of sandy, dog-friendly beach year round. Easily
accessed from the large National Trust car park (SX 676415, ///logo.
middle.decorated) it has a café and toilets. Please observe signs and
keep your dog under control.

Walk 15 Occombe Valley

Occombe Valley Woods Nature Reserve (photo opposite) is criss-
crossed with minor footpaths and bisected by a stream ideal
for dogs. The route is off-lead, apart from the first few hundred
metres. Start from Occombe Farm, with its farm shop, café and
car park (SX 876631, ///award.leap.half, signed from the A380 on
Preston Down Road, Paignton TQ3 1RN) but please note that the
gates shut at 6 pm. Leave the car park at the western end. Cross
Preston Down Road carefully. Turn right along the pavement. Turn
left PUBLIC FOOTPATH. At the foot of the slope, turn left at a gateway
and follow the valley path ahead. This may be followed for 2.5 km
(1 1/2 miles) to Preston.

Walk 16 Cockington

Cockington Country Park is signed from the Torquay to Paignton road. It comprises 450 acres of parkland, woodland, formal gardens and rural countryside. There is plenty of room for off-lead dog walks and a network of paths, plus well signed, colour-coded trails. (Download a map from www.countryside-trust.org.uk). The 2.3 km (1 1/2 mile) Estate Trail, marked with orange waymarks, is the longest of these and gives access to the Lakes Trail (0.8 km/ 1/2 mile) and two woodland trails.

Start from the Visitor Centre (SX 895639, ///visitors.jolly.uplifting) by the café, shops, thatched cottages and inn. Head over the park to historic Cockington Court. Bear left between the church and the formal gardens. Reaching a lane, turn left, then right to join the Estate Trail.

Walk 17 Baker's Park, Newton Abbot

Baker's Park is a great place to let your dog off-lead to enjoy roaming the woods and playing in the river Lemon. From the playing fields, a pleasant riverside path leads into the woods and may be followed for 2.2 km (1 1/2 miles) to Chercombe Bridge. Start from the parking area on the western side of Totnes Road (SX 853710, ///farm.props.casino, free at the time of writing, but limited to three hours). Follow the surfaced path ahead. Cross a footbridge and continue ahead over open ground and into the woods. From Chercombe Bridge you may extend the walk a further 700 m (1/2 mile) along the field path to Morley Bridge. Please stay on the footpath, which includes a stile without a dog gate.

Walk 18   Eastcliff Park, Teignmouth

Eastcliff is really three adjacent parks with convenient parking, benches and dog bins. Mules Park, the main area, is a flowery meadow ideal for letting your dog off-lead. The Rowdens contains specimen trees and more formal gardens and the Dell is a shady valley with ponds, palms and exotic shrubs. Start from Eastcliff pay-and-display car park (SX 945732, ///mills.sized.start) on the Dawlish Road. Walk through the archway at the lower end of the car park (MULES PARK) and up steps. The surfaced path continues uphill parallel to Eastcliff Walk. For the best coastal views, continue uphill on the footpath or Eastcliff Walk. (The field path has two stiles with dog gates).

Other good places for walks

19 Cann Woods

Cann Woods' Blue Trail is very well-marked and offers a pleasant 4.4 km/2 3/4 mile walk through mixed woodland. Much of the trail is level, with a few modest ascents and descents. Dogs are welcome and bins are provided, but a sign asks owners to keep their pets in sight and under control as farm animals graze in neighbouring fields. Start from the Forest England car park (SX547596, ///rocky.hoping.frost) on the Boringdon Hill Road, heading north from Plympton towards Lee Moor and Shaugh Prior.

20 Orley Common, Ipplepen

Orley Common is a mosaic of ancient woodland, grassland, flowery glades and scrub. Criss-crossed with paths, it offers many possibilities for short, off-lead rambles, but please don't let your dog disturb the abundant wildlife or leave the common into adjoining fields. Start from the small car park half a mile from Ipplepen church on the minor road (Orley Road) to Torbryan (SX827666, ///pixies.originate.negotiators). Use the car park's helpful map and noticeboard to orient yourself.

Some of the best dog-friendly beaches in South Devon

South Devon has a fine collection of dog friendly beaches. As well as South Milton Sands (page 29), Soar Mill Cove (page 14); Churston Cove and Elberry Cove (page 18) and Sugary Cove (page 16), I also recommend Ayrmer Cove; North Sands, Salcombe; Gara Rock; North Hallsands; Beesands, Slapton Sands; Strete Gate; Scabbacombe; Man Sands and Maidencombe.

Full details of these and more dog-friendly beaches are in my *Devon Beach and Cove Guide.*